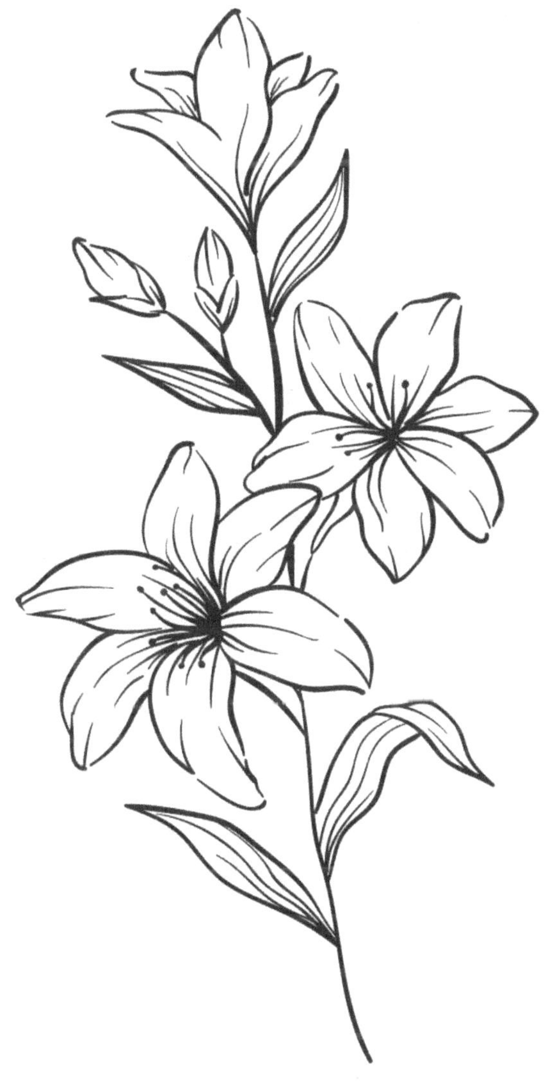

contents

planning wedding checklist

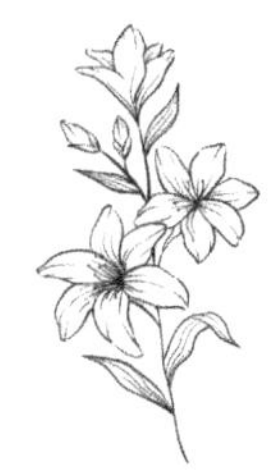

10 – 12 MONTHS before Waiting DAY(wedding day)

- ❑ Begin collecting inspiration images

- ❑ Determine the budget

- ❑ Choose a wedding date and time

- ❑ Book your ceremony location and officiant

- ❑ Define your wedding style and choose a color palette

- ❑ Begin organising addresses and names for your guest list

- ❑ Extend invitations to the bridal party

- ❑ Start researching

  suggestions for videographers, caterers,

  florists

- ❑ entertainment, photographers, etc.

- ❑ Begin looking for the dress!

- ❑ Register for your marriage license

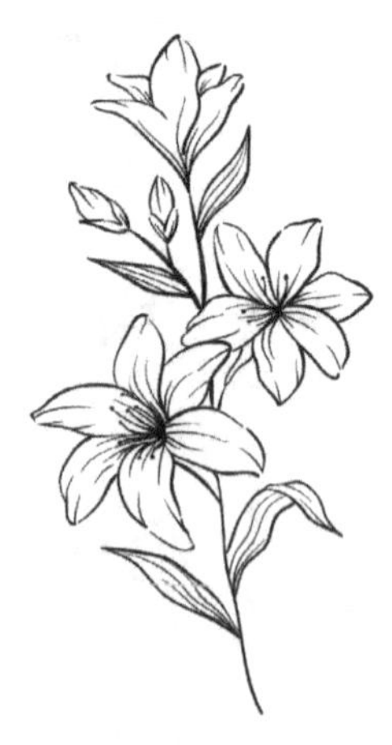

<u>8 – 10 MONTHS before THE Waiting DAY</u>

❑ Finalise the guest list

❑ Book your caterer

❑ Book your videographer and photographer

❑ Book your florist

❑ Book your ceremony musicians

❑ Book your reception entertainment

❑ Choose and order the dress

❑ Choose and order bridesmaids dresses

❑ Reserve hotel blocks for out-of-town guests

❑ Reserve a hotel for your wedding night

❑ Choose/design and order your save the dates

❑ Reserve dance floor, linens, charger plates,

linens, tables, rentals chairs

❑ Reserve day of makeup and hairstyle too

❑ Create your wedding website

6 – 8 MONTHS before THE Waiting DAY(big day)

❑ Mail your save the dates

❑ Select and order your invitation

suite

❑ Reserve your calligrapher if needed

❑ Reserve rehearsal dinner venue

❑ Book your wedding day

transportation

❑ Select and book wedding bands

❑ Book your honeymoon! Secure

passports if needed.

❑ Choose groom and groomsman attire

❑ Choose wedding favors for guests

❑ order wedding cake, and Have your cake

tasting

❑ Schedule first dress fitting. Bring your

wedding shoes!

❑ Create your wedding registry if having one.

4 – 6 MONTHS before THE Waiting DAY

❑ Send invitation suite to calligrapher if

needed

❑ Purchase or rent all groomsman attire

❑ Schedule hair and makeup trial

❑ Plan day of getting ready arrangements for a

bridal party

❑ Draft floor plans

❑ Design all printed materials with stationer

2 - 4 MONTHS before THE Waiting DAY

❑ Send invitations about 12 weeks before the

big day

❑ Schedule hair and makeup services for

a bridal party

❑ Schedule last dress fitting

❑ Finalize floral selections

❑ Have an engagement shoot

❑ Have menu tasting with the caterer

❑ Finalise catering menu

❑ Draft day-of timeline

❑ Purchase gifts for your bridal party

❑ Purchase gifts for your parents

❑ Purchase materials for out-of-town

Welcome Bags

❑ Create an order of ceremony for the officiant

❑ Choose ceremony songs and submit to

musicians

❑ prelude, processional, special songs, signing of the register, recessional, etc.

❑ Choose the special reception songs and submit them to DJ/Band introductions, parent dances, first dance, last dance, cake cutting, etc.

❑ Purchase details for the ceremony and guest book, confetti basket, reception ring pillow, and pens, etc. programs, wedding signage, menu card, map, table plan, table names, etc.

6 WEEKS before THE WEDDING DAY

❑ Print and complete all day-of printed

materials

❑ Write your vows if desired

❑ Collect all RSVP's and create a seating plan

for reception

❑ Submit final guest count to suppliers

❑ Modify and confirm rental quantities

needed

❑ Confirm honeymoon travel arrangements

1 MONTH before THE WEDDING DAY

- ❏ Update the day-of timeline

- ❏ Send final payments to suppliers

- ❏ Create a shot list complete with friends and names of family you want in each image for your photographer

- ❏ Send the final guest list in alphabetical order with seating assignments to caterer

- ❏ Give final guarantee to a caterer and include any dietary restrictions

2 WEEKS before THE WEDDING DAY

❑ Get final hair cut and color!

❑ Finalise the Day of a timeline and send it to all

 suppliers

❑ Send a day of schedules to your bridal party

❑ Confirm all suppliers

❑ Have your final venue walkthrough

1 WEEK before THE WEDDING DAY

❑ Confirm wedding day transportation

schedules

❑ Designate someone to take the gifts home

after the big day

❑ Designate someone to take all wedding

decor

❑ Designate someone returns rentals that

are not picked up on the wedding night

❑ Put cash payments in envelopes and label

❑ Oversee marquee setup if marquee

wedding

1 DAY before THE WEDDING DAY

- ❑ Drop of materials to the reception venue

- ❑ Drop off welcome bags at the

  hotel/accommodation

- ❑ Give your planner/chosen person any cash

  payments for them to distribute. on the day

  to suppliers

THE WEDDING DAY!

❏ Enjoy every minute of your wedding

day!

❏ Eat breakfast, lunch and snacks!

❏ Remember your marriage is what

matters most!

AFTER THE WEDDING DAY

❑ Enjoy your honeymoon!

❑ Send thank-you notes to suppliers

❑ Send thank-you notes for wedding gifts

❑ Have your wedding dress cleaned and

preserved

❑ Order your wedding photo prints &

enjoy the memories forever.

10 Outdoor Wedding Mistakes to Avoid

if you are considering getting married outdoors here's a list of 10 things that you need to consider if you are having an outdoor wedding :

❖ number one: is rain do not ignore the rain and do not ignore the possibility of rain I know a lot of brides are like well if I don't have a rain plan then it's not gonna happen or we'll figure it out.

if you do decide that you'll hurry up and get married like if it's sprinkling or something and then you don't have any music also you might want to check with your band to make sure that they don't need a tent some of them might bring their own but if not you can rent a tent for them and just make sure that you have it covered in case it rains so that you can still get married outside if that's something that you really want to do, so just be sure that you're checking your contracts with your venue and your entertainment and so that you know what it looks like if it does rain.

❖ number two: the extreme temperatures whether it's hot or cold if it is going to be cold or there's a possibility that it could be a little chilly, you will want to have heaters and blankets available and then if it is going to be hot you want to make sure that your guests aren't just sitting there sweating. so I recommend doing fans if you even do paper fans it doesn't seem like it but those do actually make a big difference, and also I highly recommend having water somewhere right near your ceremony so that they can cool off and have a drink while they're waiting for you to walk down the aisle. you might also want to have a plan here if it's just too hot or just too cold to move your ceremony or your reception inside especially if you're getting married somewhere like Colorado where you have no idea what you're going to get like in October so just have a plan and know what your options are that will save you a ton of stress on your wedding day and it will also make the experience much more enjoyable for both you and your guests.

❖ number three: bugs oh my gosh you want to make sure you are covered if you are getting married near the water, there are going to be a ton of mosquitoes. mosquitoes can have a really big impact on the experience of your big day, you don't want your guests or your bridal party or yourself fighting off mosquitoes in the middle of your ceremony and if the reception is gonna be outside as well you don't want people outside getting eaten alive the whole night I recommend offering bug spray there's also a little like towelettes you can get that you could hand out before the ceremony. the other thing that can cause major issues with bugs is if there are animals at your venue there are a lot of cool venues that are like rustic barns or maybe you're getting married at the zoo or something like that, but where there are animals there are flies and flies are miserable to deal with especially if you are having an outdoor reception so if it is really important to you to have like an outdoor reception and have your entire wedding outside I recommend going with something that is not going to have animals present so that you don't have to worry about the Flies all night.

❖ number four: that you definitely need to consider if you're having an outdoor wedding is the wind so many times, I have been fighting the wind at the ceremony because if you're having your ceremony outside and there's a chance that it could be windy I would recommend against any paper like fliers or programs or anything this is not something that you want to be fighting also, if you are going to have your reception outside or at least your like cocktail hour with your escort cards be sure that your escort cards can blow away there's nothing worse than sitting there fighting the escort cards trying to get them to the guests before the wind blows them away. if your reception is outside be sure that the escort cards that are on the table are weighted, make sure that everything is weighted especially if you do like some frames sitting up or anything like that just make sure that it's all taken care of also if you have a bunch of draping you'll want to make sure that it is tied down like near the bottom so that you don't have to worry about it flying everywhere.

- ❖ number five: your shoes and your bridesmaid shoes if you are walking down grass or a dirt aisle you do not want to be wearing stilettos. I don't care how amazing they are they always look ridiculous if you are sinking into the ground and struggling to walk down the aisle, it is so not worth it if you do have an amazing pair of stilettos that you want to wear and you do have a grassy aisle or something maybe put those on for the reception, but choose a different pair of shoes like a pair of wedges or something for the ceremony it's just not worth it to struggle down the aisle, it does not look good and it's stressful.
- ❖ number six: the sunscreen you do not want to sit there and get fried during your ceremony and during your photos that is just not going to be a good look and you're going to be totally uncomfortable, so it's great to just apply a little bit of sunscreen while you're getting ready to make sure that you're covered and you're not gonna get burnt, and then you might also want to do the little sunscreen towelettes or offer a little sunscreen for your guests as well if you know that it's going to be very sunny or very hot.

❖ number seven: the sound, a lot of outdoor venues have sounds that are uncontrollable so whether that's road noise it might be like a waterfall or whatever or maybe other people are around if there's any chance of your ceremony being drowned out by other sounds you'll want to make sure that you have mics on your ceremony just so that everybody can hear and they can actually be there with you and enjoy the moment, and people aren't like what what what do you say. I've seen that happen too many times there's like an amazing water feature or something at a venue and then it just completely drowns out the couple's voices I kind of recommend just getting a microphone anyway at least having your efficient mic so that your voice kind of carry into the microphone, especially if you're getting married outside you want to make sure that you have the sound covered so that everybody can hear you.

❖ number eight: umbrellas or coverings so if there's a chance of rain or really hot Sun you want to make sure that your guests have somewhere they can go to hide out if they need to especially if they are sitting there waiting for you to walk down the aisle or something like that you just want to make sure that everyone's comfortable so offering umbrellas is great if there's a good chance of rain or just having somewhere like near the ceremony where people can get out of the weather if they need to.

❖ number nine: uneven terrain I already kind of mentioned this when I said you need to make sure you have the right shoes but the other important thing that this impact is your older guests if you have older guests who might have trouble walking, you want to make sure that you have somebody to escort them or maybe like a golf cart or something to help them, if there's going to be uneven terrain you don't want to have your old grandma having to hike through a bunch of rocks or grassy hills. so be sure that you consider the older folks and make sure that there's somebody there to help them if needed and then also obviously make sure that if you know there's any even terrain that you pick the right shoes for yourself in for the bridal party so that nobody bites the dust' while they're walking down the aisle because that would be super embarrassing it, would be funny and it would be a good story later, but you just don't want to do that, so yes make sure that you walk the ceremony area when you are doing your venue walkthrough and pay attention to the terrain and make sure that it's going to be okay for both you and your older guests.

- number ten: restrooms, where are the restrooms if you're getting married outside, be sure that you consider the restrooms when you have like 150 to 200 people in an area they are going to need a restroom but you want to make sure that you have it available for them to use as well as signage marking where the restroom is, so that you're not answering the question of where is the bathroom on your wedding day, you want to make sure that it's readily available and nearby also, you want to know when you're booking your venue if you're going to book an outdoor venue, be sure you ask them about the restroom options you don't want to find out later that you have to have your guests use an outhouse, that's very fun to find out so make sure you're asking that question when you're booking your outdoor venue, make sure that restrooms are available because this will definitely impact the experience for you and your guests. so the outdoors can be a little bit unpredictable but if you just take these things into consideration and make sure that you're covered it's going to be amazing.

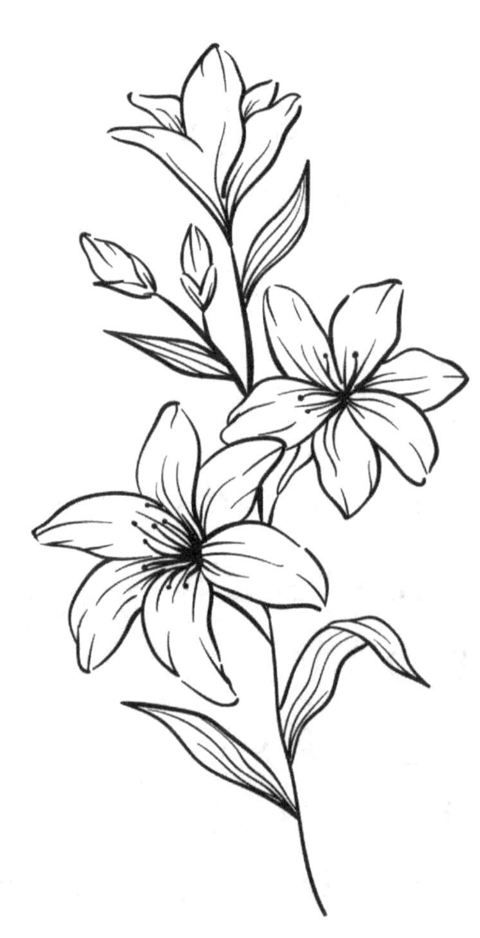

How to calculate your wedding planning budget

the first big thing that you have to think about when trying to project what your overall weddings costs are going to be are your guest count numbers. I know this is the hardest thing to think about. A lot of my clients are really struggling in the beginning of the process. Coming up with a number of how many people they're going to invite and how many people will actually attend. The literature on the internet these days says you should expect about 80% of your guests to say yes that you invite and 20% to say no. I strongly disagree with this number. You should be expecting more like 90 to 95% of your guests to attend. So you want to be sure that those guest count numbers, people that you actually invite are those that you want to attend your event. It is so common these days for people to be responding yes, so you have to be sure that you're inviting people that you definitely want to be there to support you on your big day. Skip the courtesy invites, people. It's just not worth it. So, first things first, your guest count. You need to get together first, once you're

engaged and you're reveling in all of the good juju that everybody's sending your way, congratulations by the way,
it is so imperative of you to sit down with your fiance with both sides of the family and discuss who is on the must invite list. Your A list group of people, The people that you all know and agree have to attend the event, Now, there's going to be, very likely, some overlap between your list, with your fiance, your list with your parents and your fiance's list with their parents, okay. So everybody, all three of these sort of parties should start making their wish list of all the people that they know that they need to invite. From there, you need to whittle that list down to find out where the overlap is, And then come up with a condensed version of who you're inviting overall and get your big grand number. Now, the number of guests that you invite to your wedding, 90 to 95% of those guests are very likely to attend. This is the number one driving factor of your budget is the number of guests that you have. You can't get away without feeding and watering all of your people, The biggest check you're going to write is for food and

beverage, the number of guests that you invite and also the number of guests that actually attend are going to be the single driving factor of your budget. The next part of this formula and equation, to gauge how much your wedding is actually going to cost you is your overall budget target range. because a lot of clients that I talk to early on in the process come to me and say, we don't have a number, I'm sorry everybody has a number, Don't give me this line. You have a number in mind that you roughly know is your freak out number, the number you don't want to spend more than, because it's just going to freak you out.

Your number might be different than your parents' number or your fiance's number, so now's the time to have this discussion with those that are contributing. What is the freak out number? That's going to be the high end of your range. The lower end of your range is going to be determined by the number of contributing parties that you have. I often see these days, that couples together are contributing to their overall budget, and then one partner's parents or family members might also be contributing. The other partners might be contributing.

Forget the rules of the past. There's so many different contributing factors here, And keep in mind that people that are financially contributing to your event will also really have some leverage to have decision making power, So be sure that you're okay with that, too. Now, we're going to do a little bit of math. I think in colors, not numbers, so bear with me here. You want to take the number of guests that you're inviting, so, let's say that's 100 guests just to keep nice round numbers for the math challenged, 100 guests and your overall target budget is $100,000. That's the high end of your range, that's your freak out number. So here, you want to divide your overall target budget number, $100,000, you want to divide that number by the number of guests that you're inviting. Divide that by 100.
You're going to come up with your price per person. I want you to shift all of your thinking away from, that was a $75,000 wedding, that was $100,000 wedding, that was a million dollar wedding, I want you to erase everything that you think you know about what budgets are for certain weddings that you see on Pinterest or online. None of the overall target budget numbers matter for any wedding that you ever come across if you do not also know the guest count,

This is imperative because a $100,000 wedding, for example, for 100 people looks very different from a $100,000 wedding for 500 people. So, the difference here is the price per person is the critical number that you want to get to, This is going to be really informative for you throughout the entire planning process and making decisions and asking questions of your vendors before you book them to find out whether they are going to be within reach for you given your budget numbers, This is so important. Forget everything that you think you know about overall target budgets and boil it down to the price per person, What's the overall budget and how many guests attended, Divide the number of the target overall budget, your freak out number, divide that number by the number of guests that you're inviting, to be conservative. Thinking that 90 to 95% of your guests will attend, notice I'm not asking you to divide it by the 90 to 95 number. We're going to be conservative and just bank it on all of the people coming, which is not going to happen, but you'll get a figure of a price per person. So, here we are. $100,000 target budget and 100 guests. Okay, that is $1,000 per person. let me break it down for you, You have to understand that the numbers that I'm using are just an example, and I'm not saying you should be spending this, I am just using a nice, round number so we can operate from a place of ease of calculation, if you will.

Your budget is going to be different. Your guest count is going to be much, much different. Anyway, so we have $1,000 per person, And here's what that means. You're at least going to spend around $200 per person on a professional caterer with several courses for a seated dinner, at least $200 per person on food. The driving factor of the budget is your food and beverage bill. You're going to have to feed and water these people. So that's $200 per person for food. Let's say another $20 to $30-ish for your bar for call brands, Let's say $50 per person for a premium bar package. These are ranges, I'm not saying that this is standard across the entire nation coast to coast. These are numbers I'm familiar with and the kinds of weddings that we're doing in my local market, so yours may vary slightly one way or the other. This is just for an example, for us to walk through this as an exercise. So, let's say we're at $200 per person for food, $50 per person for the most premium bar package ever, that's $250 per person, just on food and beverage. Okay, the biggest check that you're going to write, You're going to have a venue spend to rent out the venue. If you have a ceremony and a reception in multiple places that's two venue expenses. Let's say anywhere between $6,000 and $8,000 for both of those, okay. That is six to eight percent of the $100,000 budget. If you have $250 per person and you have 100 guests, we're looking at 25% of your budget right there, 25% is gone on food and beverage, We have six to eight percent on the venue alone. Now, if you have a seated dinner or if you have a cocktail style reception, these numbers on your rentals are going to vary a little bit. With a seated dinner, you're seating 100% of your guests, tables for everybody, chairs for everybody, linens on every table, arrangements on every table, place settings at every place setting, plate sets, flatware, that's glassware, that's bread and butter. We're talking about all in. You might think that these details are minutia that just really aren't all that important. I guarantee you this adds up so quickly. When you have 100 guests, you have to have this for all 100 of your guests for a seated dinner. Now, cocktail style reception, it's not as expensive on the rental side, because you don't

have to have chairs for everybody, tables for everybody, linens on every table, times 100 guests. You don't have to have that. You might gauge 80% of those guests or even 60% in some cases.
That all depends on how much square footage your venue holds. Those two things are going to vary a little bit in the cost of rentals, but you can see how it's already adding up. Then you're going to have a band, which is several thousand dollars, or a DJ which is a couple hundred to maybe a couple of thousand dollars, too, depending on what kind of DJ you go for and how many hours your reception is. you're also going to have a photographer. You might have a videographer. Both of those things you can expect to spend a couple of thousand dollars on at least. But if you really value photography and also videography, you might spend a little bit more. Those are very splurge-worthy items because these are the deliverables you physically will have for the rest of your life from your event day, Worth the splurge on both of these things. We haven't even talked flowers. So, depending on how big your bridal party is, imagine that you're going to have to give a bouquet to every single person at your bridal party.

All the more reason to not have a massive bridal party. And because you have to boutonniere for your guys, bouquets for the girls, That adds up really fast, The bigger the bridal party, the bigger the floral bill. But if you do a ceremony chuppah or some sort of ceremony alters the arrangement, that is an expense. And let me tell you, this is something that is a statement piece, so that might be a couple of thousand dollars, Decor, and design, your flowers, especially candles, any other lighting arrangements that you have coming in to really enhance the space, that is a huge range. This is where a lot of the flex with your budget is going to come in, your biggest check you're going to write is for food and beverage. You can certainly write a really big check for decor if you wanted to, but I'm talking in general terms here. That part of your budget is going to range based on your personal taste.

you're in control of whatever that is, I recommend you carve out all the must-have items first before you determine what your design budget should be because that is where you have flex to make that bigger if you have more budget that frees itself up,or make it smaller, as small as you necessarily need to have it given whatever your constraints are with your bridal party,

and then with the actual tables on your floor plan if you're doing a seated dinner versus a cocktail style reception, Equipment for your band or your DJ. You'll need a stage, possibly a dance floor, You need to check your band's writer to see if you have a backline that you need to supply or if the band's supplying their own, Whether that's additional or that's included in their cost.

All things you need to consider, so band, photo, video, catering, your venue, the big five. Those five things are really, really big. You got to book those early on and those are going to eat up the biggest part of your budget, Floral decor, lighting decor, rentals, if you do specialty rentals, like upgrading your chairs from your venue. Maybe you're going to bring in lounge seating arrangements for around the dance floor. Or maybe outside you want to do specialty bars with fancy bar backs. All of these things are decor items that all add up, that's all part of the flex. And we're talking about a $100,000 overall budget and 100 guests, and that $1,000 per person, what does that look like?

That is for somebody, in my experience, that does enhance the space with quite a bit of decor, so flowers, rentals, lighting elements to really juj up space if you will. Those sorts of things are really important to clients that spend $1,000 per person. But again, that's not everybody.

Let's do something else with this exercise, Let's talk about what $100,000 looks like because you might have a really, really big guest count, Let's go up to 250, probably not going to have a seated dinner. that's a lot of people, Those large guest counts with the same budget numbers, with $100,000. Let's divide $100,000 by the number of guests, divided by 250 people that are being invited for the same overall target budget range, that freak out the number of $100,000. let's divide that, and then we come up with a new price per person of $400 per person, okay, whether it's a seated dinner or a cocktail style reception, again, that depends on a number of factors. $400 per person versus what we had already talked about at $1,000 per person, the difference here is the food and beverage number kind of stays the same. we're still looking at about $200 per person on food.

Let's pause here for a second and think about going out for a birthday party or some other thing when you are celebrating a milestone and you want to go to a nice restaurant, and you have your partner, and then maybe a couple of friends, so you have like five or six people that you all go out to dinner with. You have some drinks, you have a good meal, you have a really good time, You might pay a premium to be at a super-exclusive restaurant or something different. You're probably coming away from that restaurant experience under everyday circumstances spending about $200-ish per person on food, Maybe also including beverage. However you want to slice it, what we're talking about here is in terms that are relative to dining in general. I'm not just pulling this out and saying weddings are specifically going to cost more than what you might actually spend if you went out to a nice restaurant on a nice occasion with a group of people, and this is what you're looking at. Back to our math. So, 250 people divided into $100,000 is $400 per person. We're still looking at about $200 per person on food, maybe a premium bar package is not really where you're going to go here for this because the budget really is a little

more constrained than in our last equation. So, we're looking at maybe a lesser package, so like $35 per person, for not necessarily your premium bar service package. So all in for food and beverage here. We're doing $235 per person-times, 250 people.
what does this look like?
That gets us at just under $60,000 per person, okay. We're at $58,750 and we haven't even talked about the fact that you still have to add in taxes and gratuities, 20% is typical gratuity added on to catering bill, And then tax is roughly 10% let's say adding another 30% to the food and beverage bill. That's a big part of the $100,000 budget, You'll definitely be getting a DJ for less than $1,000. You're definitely getting a photographer for just a couple of thousand dollars. You're investing in just what's included in your venue, with linens and rentals and things like that so you can keep your rental cost down, When you factor in tax and gratuity on your catering bill and your catering bill starts at $58,750, food and beverage for 250 people, we're already at $76,000. So you have a little less than $24,000 to go to everything else for your event. Not saying it can't happen. It happens all the time. But I'm showing you

the difference here between when you have $100,000 for 100 people and when you have $100,000 for 250 people. It is very very different here from what you're working with.

And the first biggest chunk of change you need to take out of that budget number before you determine what your Pinterest inspiration is going to be, 'cause Pinterest is not really very informative for you in terms of what those arrangements are actually going to cost, what the labor is for all those things. All of those decor items should come after you've factored in food and beverage, tax and gratuity, your venue, your photographer, your entertainment because you have to have those things, And then everything else is nice to have but not need to have. You don't need to have favors for everybody, You don't need to have programs, these things you have to really consider after you've taken out the big chunks of your overall budget calculation. So, that way you can go through the planning process with a very educated expectation on what you should spend in a given category. Forget all of the things that you're seeing online from different publications posting how much you should expect to spend on a wedding.

None of them are scientifically gathered, None of them are accurate, They are based on self-reporting from people all over the country and there is no single controlling factor or variable here that you can rely on for this information to even be applicable to you in your notes. The one thing I'm telling you that you can is the price per person, taking that overall target budget into consideration.

Wedding Advice from 8 REAL Brides!

✓ **1:wedding advice**

"don't try to accomplish everything at

once or you will just get overwhelmed.

don't forget to eat on your beautiful wedding

day.

it's easy not to because you get so

busy with everything but you end up

light-headed and dizzy."

✓ **2:wedding regret**

"not having a wedding planner. I

wish have had more help. doing everything

Click to add text

the day of sucks and

it's stressful"

✓ **3:wedding advice**

"take a moment with

your husband alone. the day goes by so

quickly that you should have five minutes at

least to see each other talk, and have no

one else around. we had several occasions to

do that and

it slowed down the day and helped us

cherish each other."

✓ **4:wedding advice**

"things will go wrong. just make sure that

people don't tell you about them until

the next day. I told everyone that was helping

just fix it and keep me clueless."

✓ **5:wedding regret**

"smaller guest list. It's true when they say that's how you cut costs the most. looking back I would have cut my list down quite a bit, saving money on invitations, food, etc, etc..."

✓ **6:wedding advice**

"even if you think that you

have what you need and live together.

you can always use

towels, throw blankets, tools, etc.

think outside of the box."

✓ **7:wedding regret**

"A videographer. I really

wish we would have gotten a

videographer."

✓ **8:wedding regret**

" Our photographer was inexpensive but in our work, it showed my husband and I don't have one single
picture of just us two. We definitely would have spent more for better photos and have we had known that."

important names and numbers:

ceremony venue _______________________________________

reception venue_______________________________________

coordinator/wedding planner ____________________________

caterer____

officiant ____

photographer____

videographer____

cake/desserts____

lighting ____

hair____

makeup ____

tailor____

rentals ____

flowers____

dress salon____

rehearsal dinner venue______________________________________

transportation______________________________________

stationery/paper goods______________________________________

VIP/best person______________________________________

VIP/best person______________________________________

VIP/alternate best person______________________________________

other______________________________________

other______________________________________

other______________________________________

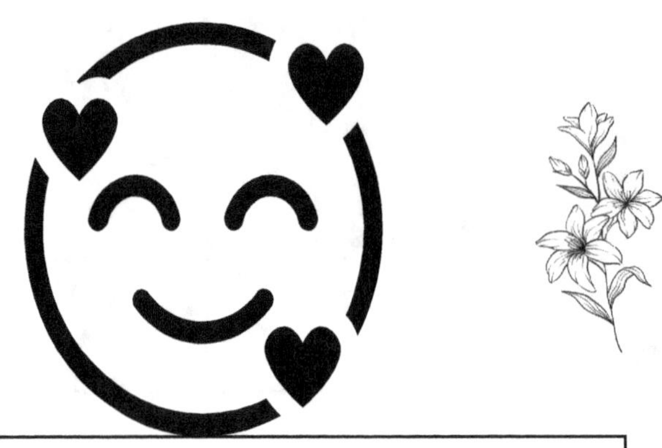

Congratulation

on your wedding!!

wishing you everlasting love, joy,

and happiness just like unending

circles of your wedding rings!

may the years ahead be filled with

lasting joy

your wedding day will come and go,

but may your love forever grow

May this new start, bring all the joy

and happiness in your life.

May you always stay in love with

each other. Enjoy your wedding day.

<u>*Notes:*</u>...

....

....

....

....

....

....

....

....

....

....

....

....

Notes:..

Notes:..

....

....

....

....

....

....

....

....

....

....

....

....

....

Notes:...

....

....

....

....

....

....

....

....

....

....

....

....

Notes:...

Notes:..

....

....

....

....

....

....

....

....

....

....

....

....

Notes:..

Notes:..

60

Notes:...

Notes:...

Notes:...

Notes:...

....

....

....

....

....

....

....

....

....

....

....

Notes:..

Notes:..

Notes:..

67

Notes:..

Notes:..

....

....

....

....

....

....

....

....

....

....

....

Notes:..

....

....

....

....

....

....

....

....

....

....

....

www.ingramcontent.com/pod-product-compliance
Lightning Source LLC
Chambersburg PA
CBHW060519120726
48002CB00011B/3236